HOW TO GET STARTED IN EXPORTING – A $243 BILLION MARKET

REVISED EDITION

The Dun & Bradstreet Business Library

New York
Thomas Y. Crowell Company
Established 1834

Manufactured in the United States of America

L.C. Card 78-132309
ISBN 0-690-41247-9

1 2 3 4 5 6 7 8 9 10

1549410

Contents

Foreword

World trade, as the name implies is something which involves all the nations of the world. It has been going on for centuries. In its simplest form, it consists of the buying and selling of goods and services across national borders. As new developments in transportation and communications have come about to bring people and markets closer, world trade has grown greatly, and the volume of exports and imports continues to expand.

A country exports those products that it can produce better or cheaper than the buying country. It imports those items that it either does not have, (such as certain raw materials) or cannot make, at less cost than someone else. In addition to this fairly obvious exchange of goods, a considerable two-way trade has developed in various consumer items that people buy simply because they like them.

1

For the United States, trade is vital to our economic well being. Imports provide the wide variety of raw materials needed by industry, while exports enable our farms and factories to expand production and make more sales. World trade also provides jobs in factories, on farms, and in the many transportation companies, ports, banks and other service organizations which are involved in the sale, shipment and financing of these goods and services.

CHAPTER 1

Introduction to Export

Export is no get-rich-quick scheme, nor is it a way to dispose of left-over products! It is something to be taken seriously—with profits to match the energy and effort you put into it.

Although export, like domestic business, consists of selling and serving customers, the big difference is that in export, buyer and seller are separated by national borders and are often oceans apart.

This means that the supplier in the United States has to be aware that communications time and transportation time are generally longer than in domestic business. He also has to remember that he must abide by the laws and trade practices of both his own and his customer's country, and that there is frequently a difference in language.

To the non-exporter, this makes export look far too complicated to be worth bothering with. Is it worth the effort? There are quite a few United States companies, both large and small, who know it is!

In 1969, free world exports amounted to $243 billion. According to the United Nations experts who did the figuring, in the last five years, the volume of trade has grown by 60%. That's a lot of business by any standard and it clearly demonstrates that there are real profit opportunities for anyone who wants to sell in the world market place—a market place consisting of some 3.5 billion people, about 3.3 billion of them outside the United States. It's a constantly growing market place, with more and more potential customers appearing every day. By 1975, world population is expected to climb to nearly 4 billion.

Although the United States is the world's leading trading nation, it is still not doing as well in export as it should. While United States exports in 1969 hit an all-time high of $37.3 billion in recent years, our share of total trade has declined from 18.3% to 14.7%. In other words, although the world trade pie keeps getting bigger, our slice gets smaller.

There are a number of reasons why our exports are not expanding at the same rate as are those of other countries —Japan's share of world exports in the last ten years grew from 2.4 to 4.8%; Italy's rose from 2.1 to 3.9% and Germany's share went from 7.5 to 9.9%—but the basic reason is that too many American companies have, for too long, completely ignored overseas profit opportunities. While the figures vary on just how many U.S. firms are actively engaged in export, it is generally accepted that only about 5% of the American companies who could export do so.

Why this lack of interest in export? Because of the real need for more American exports (to help correct our serious balance of payments deficit), for the past several years the United States Government has been actively carrying out a National Export Expansion Program. The objective of this program is to help those who are engaged in export expand their overseas business and to convince the nonexporters that they should start exporting. In supporting this program, the late President Kennedy had this to say: "More exports will mean a stronger America, a more prosperous America; and greater assurance of a free world." President Nixon has said: "In the coming years, our economic stability and the continuing progress of free nations of the world will require us, as never before, to further increase the flow of U.S. goods to international markets."

Former President Johnson was also a strong supporter of exports, noting: "Our success in creating and satisfying the demands of our domestic market has brought our country to its present high level of opportunity. Often, however, the very opportunities we found at home caused us to neglect other promising markets overseas. Exports benefit all Americans. They stimulate business by providing new outlets for its industrial capacity. They benefit labor and help in the war on poverty by creating more jobs. Every $1 billion increase in our exports results in 100,000 new jobs for Americans. Although we are selling substantial amounts of our products abroad, we ought to do better. World trade is increasing and our share of this trade has not kept pace with our nation's capacity to produce what other countries need and are able to buy. The opportunities are there. We cannot afford to neglect them for lack of knowledge or interest."

This lack of knowledge or interest is the real nub of the problem; and to make it a bit more difficult, there is a holdover from the past of suspicion and distrust of anything foreign. Fortunately, in the last few years, with the new developments in transportation and communications, the world has become smaller and many Americans are discovering that our friends abroad are no longer quite as different or "foreign" as they once seemed to be. They have likes and dislikes similar to our own. They want products and services that will enable them to enjoy a better way of life, and in most cases they have the means to pay for what they want.

It is obvious that national interest dictates immediate strong efforts to expand exports. The profit opportunities are real enough to motivate business and yet many companies still do not investigate world markets. Why don't more companies tackle export? In a number of cases it is because they are misinformed. Under the National Export Expansion Program, one of the things the Government (through the United States Department of Commerce and the Regional Export Expansion Councils) is doing, is to try to dispel certain myths that have sprung up about export. Among these are:

A. THE MYTH OF HIGH WAGES. People say that our high wages price us out of overseas markets. The fact is that 80% of our exports of manufactured goods come from our 10 highest-wage industries.

B. THE MYTH OF BAD CREDIT. The fact is that credit losses in overseas markets are no higher than they are in the domestic markets.

C. THE MYTH OF RED TAPE. This is no myth, but the Field Offices of the Department of Commerce can tell us how to cut red tape.

D. THE MYTH THAT AMERICAN GOODS WON'T SELL ABROAD. This country exports more than any other country in the world.

Besides these rather tired myths, there is also the misguided, but often sincere counsel being offered in many parts of the country by so-called opinion leaders who know everything about anything. Quite often when a would-be-exporter approaches these people he is advised that export is too difficult, it's too uncertain, and you can't trust those foreigners. Fortunately, this kind of business expert is becoming rarer and rarer. The good word is spreading: Export is respectable and it can be good business. While export may not be for everybody, many companies, both small or large, can do it profitably. The important thing is not to assume that export isn't for you until you have investigated it thoroughly.

And speaking of investigating, why do companies go into export? New York State's Commerce Department has found that among the reasons frequently given as to why companies export, are the following:

1. A company will find that its domestic market is saturated, making it increasingly difficult and expensive to expand sales in areas dominated by competition. Exports provide wider markets and increase profits.

2. Exports increase the productive efficiency of a company by increasing output and spreading production throughout the year.

3. The sales of many products change with the seasons of the year, and a more even sales curve can be achieved by exporting to countries south of the Equator, where seasons are the reverse of ours.

4. Diversified markets abroad represent insurance against a cutback in the domestic economy, since it is unusual for all world markets to recede at the same time.

5. Export orders are generally substantial orders, because of the distance in miles and travel time, buyers abroad often anticipate their needs by placing orders in advance of actual requirements. Increased production achieved through advanced orders may thus reduce the unit costs of the manufacturer.

6. Style or Product changes may be balanced by export markets. Many manufacturers are forced to make frequent style changes to remain competitive at home. Overseas markets, where tastes may not change as rapidly, can provide ready markets for current production while new products or new models are being introduced in the home market. (As a matter of fact, some manufacturers continue to make particular items for overseas customers long after these items have been replaced by new products in the domestic market).

7. Exports may mean the difference between overall company profit and loss. Since a company's profit often comes from the last 10 or 15% of sales, exports frequently represent the profit margin on a firm's total production.

In addition to these general reasons why companies export, here are two specific answers given to the editor of the "Trade Expansion News" published by the Committee of American Steamship Lines (now merged with the American Institute of Merchant Shipping), when he asked businessmen, "Why do you export?" The first reply is from a manufacturer of pipes, couplers, pumps and sprinklers. His reason: "We only operate full tilt three months of the year—May, June and July. The summer months are the only time our products are in demand in the domestic market. I need a year-round business, so naturally I am looking at the world as one big market." The second answer comes from a company making magnetic dies. It has been exporting for 20 years: "Our company needs an increase in overall sales volume to make a profit. Exporting gives us that margin of profit. Rising costs at home have reduced our profits and we look to overseas markets to keep us in the black."

List three reasons why your company could benefit from increased sales through export.

1. _____

2. _____

3. _____

By now, we hope the reader has gotten to the point where he will concede that maybe there is something to export after all. He may now be ready to ask: "Where's the action? How do we get in on it?"

Where's the action? It's going on right now in all the world's markets.

CHAPTER 2

All the World's Markets

The world has about 220 individual markets. Some are big, some small; Japan is a market of about 100 million people; West Germany, 59 million; Argentina, 22 million; Italy, 58 million; Mexico, 41 million; Denmark, 5 million; Iran, 24 million; France, 49 million, etc. Most of these markets have different cultures, tastes, business methods and economies. Some have a common language and some a similar way of life. Some are not really single markets, but represent a number of different markets within national borders. In certain cases, language, not nationality, plays an important role in determining markets. For example, in parts of Europe, a common language binds cities or market areas on two sides of a national boundary into a single market. In many countries there is also a difference between urban and rural markets. Religion can also play an important part in the make up of a market. Some markets are part of a larger market unit, such as the European Common Market or the Central American Common Market, and have to be considered in relation to the group and whatever trade restrictions or regulations apply to non-member nations.

Not only do markets differ as to size and membership in regional trading blocs, they also differ as to rate of development. Some are highly industrialized, such as Japan, Canada, South Africa and many in Europe. A great number of the world's markets, however, are classified as developing (or underdeveloped). Often the economies of these nations are based on the production and export of a small number of agricultural products, or as in the case of some, on the export of petroleum or other raw materials. The degree of industrialization frequently indicates the kinds of products most readily saleable in the market. The needs of the developing countries are obviously broader than may be the case in the industrialized nations, but generally their purchases are restricted by their inability to pay for all they would like to buy. The industrial nations, on the other hand, although frequently producing and exporting products similar to those made in the United States, are our best customers and can well afford a wide range of United States products.

12

Are your products best suited for industrialized countries, or developing countries? Are they for consumer use or for use by industry, agriculture, transportation, or other segments? Are they most likely to find customers in countries with climatic conditions similar to those in the United States? Take a few minutes to summarize these particulars about your products.

_____

_____

_____

_____

_____

_____

_____

_____

It is worth noting that there are a number of forces at work today re-shaping markets. At the international level, financial and technical assistance from the United Nations, the World Bank (International Bank for Reconstruction and Development), the Inter-American Bank and AID (Agency for International Development) and others, are all helping to make big changes in many markets. Loans from these sources are being used to help build new transportation and power networks, create new roads, extend water distribution, build new industrial plants and diversify agricultural production. At the national level, many governments are helping their citizens to achieve a better way of life through programs aimed at creating new industries and building homes, schools, stores, offices and factories. They are also developing new tourist facilities and opening new land to farming. Many such programs are designed to attract private foreign investment to join with local interests to hasten economic development. At the industry or business level, vast changes are taking place as local and foreign investors build or expand plants to satisfy new demands. Supermarkets are growing in number in market after market and are changing consumer buying habits. All of these developments are contributing to the ferment in the market that has to be considered when drawing up marketing plans. Anyone hoping to do business in the world marketplace has to be aware that such changes are continually taking place and must be able to understand their current and future impact on both local and foreign suppliers. Regardless of size, rate of development, or overall economic well being, each country represents a potential market for a variety of products and the successful supplier realizes that he must

know the differences that exist among them if he is going
to make sales.

One of the basic differences between markets is their
ability to buy American products. If we look at the record
for 1968 (as compiled by the United States Department
of Commerce), we find that there were 42 foreign markets
each of which bought more than 100 million dollars worth
of United States products. Add Puerto Rico to this list and
we have the top 43 markets for United States exporters.
In addition, another 23 markets each bought between
50 and 100 million dollars worth of our goods. Together
these 66 markets accounted for over 90 percent of the
total United States exports of 34 billion dollars in 1968.

Among the leading 43 markets, with Canada 'way out
in front, we find that 12 are in Europe, 12 in Latin America, 12 in Asia, 4 in the Mid-East and 2 in Africa. (See full
list on following page.) Since these 66 markets are cur-
rently the ones buying the most from the United States,
they are obviously the key markets for any company to
look into. However, it would be a mistake to overlook the
remaining markets, for several of the smaller markets may
often provide more business when added together than
any one of the large ones and by spreading your business
across a number of markets you avoid the possibility of a
complete cutback in sales, should one of the big ones have
a setback.

U.S. EXPORT RANKING

(Millions of dollars)

Markets Buying Over $100 Million

Rank	Country	1968	1967
1	Canada	8,058	7,165
2	Japan	2,950	2,695
3	United Kingdom	2,180	1,960
4	West Germany	1,712	1,706
5	Netherlands	1,370	1,235
6	Mexico	1,365	1,222
7	Italy	1,120	973
8	France	1,078	1,025
9	Australia	872	893
10	Belgium-Luxembourg	797	704
11	India	718	955
12	Brazil	709	547
13	Venezuela	655	587
14	Switzerland	559	430
15	Spain	519	521
16	Korea	511	414
17	South Africa	455	426
18	Sweden	439	393
19	Philippines	436	430
20	Taiwan	388	333
21	Colombia	319	218
22	Chile	307	248
23	Hong Kong	304	255
24	Pakistan	302	347
25	Argentina	281	230
26	Iran	279	246
27	Israel	279	196
28	South Vietnam	271	297
29	Turkey	267	252
30	Denmark	206	205
31	Peru	196	258
32	Saudi Arabia	187	169
33	Thailand	186	164
34	Indonesia	169	68
35	Bahamas	165	153
36	Jamaica	147	126
37	Greece	142	143

continued

16

U.S. EXPORT RANKING

(Millions of dollars)

Markets Buying Over $100 Million

continued

Rank	Country	1968	1967
38	Norway	140	138
39	Panama	136	139
40	Dominican Republic	115	97
41	Libya	115	86
42	New Zealand	114	90
	PLUS PUERTO RICO		

U.S. EXPORT RANKING

(Millions of dollars)

Markets Buying Over $50 Million

Rank	Country	1968	1967
1	Ecuador	98	99
2	Guatemala	94	91
3	Kuwait	92	110
4	Yugoslavia	90	96
5	Netherlands Antilles	89	78
6	Ireland	87	77
7	Portugal	86	75
8	Lebanon	83	55
9	Poland	82	61
10	Honduras	75	71
11	Costa Rica	74	64
12	Bermuda	63	57
13	Trinidad & Tobago	62	60
14	Nicaragua	62	70
15	El Salvador	61	60
16	Soviet Union	58	60
17	Ghana	56	43
18	Nigeria	56	64
19	Bolivia	55	59
20	Malaysia	54	49
21	Algeria	53	33
22	Finland	52	59
23	Congo	51	49

Where can you learn more about all the world's markets? There are quite a few sources (see Chapter VIII) such as the United States Department of Commerce, the United Nations, banks, transportation companies, publications such as Exporters' Encyclopaedia, Business Abroad, International Commerce, numerous trade associations, chambers of commerce, and state trade development offices. Among the things that a supplier needs to know about an overseas market are the following:

1. Market location, area, language, population.
2. Economic factors, such as natural resources, industrial development, overall economic health of market, income levels.
3. Access to market—import restrictions, exchange control, marking and labeling regulations.
4. Market requirements—method of measurement used, English or metric; electric current; need for special packing; trade practices.
5. Market potential; current trade figures; competition.
6. Distribution patterns; trade channels.
7. Inland transportation; ports; airports.
8. Transportation from the United States to the market.

Besides knowing where to sell, it is just as important to know how to sell, in overseas markets. There are a number of factors that can have a direct bearing on a company's sales success abroad—things such as having a good knowledge of living standards and way of life of the potential customer. Despite the very real poverty in many countries, much of the world is going middle class. New developments in communications and transportation are working to develop potential customers for a wide range of products that only a few years ago seemed unattainable to many people abroad. Not only must you be aware of these new developments in living standards and buying habits, but you also have to pay attention to such other market factors as climatic and geographical conditions, for they too can influence sales. So, too, can other things. Often the color or the packaging of a product, particularly a consumer product, can determine its success or failure. In some countries a yellow label is the official color for poison. In other markets, blue is a favorite and products in that color sell better. In some cases, size can be a problem, and you may have to provide a smaller size of model than is common in the United States. You may also do better selling a simplified, or stripped-down model than the more elaborate one that sells so well here.

This business of adapting your product to fit the buyer's needs and wants is most important and cannot be stressed enough. Unless the product can be adapted to meet local requirements (for example, if an electrical product, it has to operate on the local power supply), your chances of making sales are reduced considerably.

(Sometimes product-tailoring can get a bit extreme. According to a press report, sweet potato growers in Virginia found that their products were not being well received in England because the color was wrong. British consumers were used to the pink variety and weren't buying yellow ones. In order to cash in on a potentially big market, the Virginia growers found they had to not only think pink, but grow in that color as well.)

In addition to being ever alert to the importance of product tailoring, you should also bear in mind that in some markets you may want to consider selling in smaller product units (cigarettes are still sold one at a time in some places), to build sales and increase customer familiarity with your goods. It's worth remembering that if consumers become familiar with your product when their purchase-power is low, they are more apt to keep on buying it and increase their purchases as their income goes up.

With variations, this is just as true for many industrial products. The young apprentice who learns how to use a power tool or an office machine while taking a training course given by his government or under the sponsorship of an international organization such as the United Nations, is very apt to remember the name of the equipment and have a preference for it when he gets in a position to place an order. (It is possible for United States suppliers to sell equipment to United Nations agencies and overseas governments for use in training programs by making direct contact with the respective buying offices.)

Consider your product(s) in reference to this question of product-tailoring and jot down the modification that you know you'd have to make to sell it (them) overseas, or the points that you are not sure of and would want to check.

_____

_____

_____

Besides being alert to the need for product-tailoring and being familiar with the ways in which you can introduce your product to a market (more on this in Chapter IV) you always have to remember who the foreigner is when you sell abroad. The language barrier is a big one and cannot be ignored. While it is true that English is becoming more widely used—some 70 percent of the world's mail is in English as is about 60 percent of all broadcasts—many markets can still be sold only in the local language. Not only is it essential to sell in the local language, but it is vital to have catalogs, operating instructions, and, very often, labels in the language of the country. As a matter of fact, when it comes to labels, in some countries this is an official requirement.

Take a look at both your product(s) and your promotional material and list the points (such as label requirements, size and other features) that should be investigated.

1. _____

_____

2. _____

_____

3. _____

_____

4. _____

_____

5. _____

_____

Speaking of languages, you should bear in mind that some, Spanish, for example, may not be quite the same in every market using it. You have to make certain that you do use the correct version for the particular market. Another interesting point worth noting is that languages differ as to length of sentence and number of words needed to express the same thought. This is important if you plan to use a general sales promotion piece for several markets, leaving a given amount of space for the printed message in the local language. Dillon, Agnew and Marton, Inc., well-known international sales promotional specialists, point out that copy, translated from English into German, Dutch or French, will run 15 to 20 percent longer than the English original. Your layout must be sufficiently flexible to accommodate this expansion of copy. You should also be aware of the pitfalls of amateurish or too literal translations and of the fact that there is frequently a difference in the understanding overseas of what we regard as "common expressions." One experienced international advertising practitioner, Richard Hobbs, senior vice president of Gotham-Vladimir Advertising, Inc., cautions that in Latin America it is the hen, not the goose, that lays the golden eggs, while the South American cat has two lives less than his American cousin, or a total of seven instead of nine.

In addition to using the right language for the market, you also have to remember that local customs dictate sales promotional approaches. You should not use advertising that offends, or is contrary to local likes or dislikes (example, again given by Mr. Hobbs, concerns a leading cosmetics manufacturer who—unaware that in Arab countries cut-off hands denote a convicted thief—was stopped just in time before he entered the Near Eastern market with beautifully illustrated folders in Arabic showing the Venus de Milo).

Not only is it important to have a good understanding of what you should do and how to do it in promoting sales in the market, it is also essential to have a good idea of the geography of the country. You should be aware of the distances and transportation facilities between market centers when it comes time to appoint distributors or agents. You will also want to know about ports, airports and inland transportation to make certain your shipment moves to the port best equipped to handle it and best able to serve the customer. Don't forget that in some countries inland transportation is not all that it should be and you may be able to find an alternate route to the customer that will save him time and money. When it comes to market coverage, you have to be aware of the size of the market and not expect to cover a market with one representative who may be hundreds, if not thousands, of miles away from some of your prospective customers.

Your knowledge of overseas markets should also include a general idea of the country's history and traditions because these can also have a bearing on how you should approach your sales promotion work in the market. In some markets you may find that because of the country's long association with a European country, certain trade practices have been developed that are patterned on a European way of doing business and you may find it worthwhile to use a similar approach.

Don't overlook the competition in world markets. You have to realize that your products will be competing not only with similar products from the United States and other exporting nations and perhaps local manufacture as well, but will also be competing with many other products. Since the prospective buyer has only a limited number of pesos, francs or yen to spend, he must weigh his purchases of any particular product against his total needs and wants; you have to recognize this fact of life and sell accordingly. You have to stress user benefits in your sales efforts and not expect the prospect to receive your product with the same love and understanding of it that you have.

The important thing to remember in selling in the world market place is that it is made up of many different markets and the more you can learn about them individually, the better are your chances of developing a successful international business.

CHAPTER 3

How To Get Started

If you hope to develop a successful international business, study the various methods that can be used and select the one most appropriate to your individual company needs and capabilities. There are only two ways of conducting an export business—either you do it yourself, or you let someone else do it for you.

Since it's easier to have someone else do it for you, let's consider this approach first. The simplest way to do this is to sell your products to a Buyer for Export—this may be an independent Export-Import firm, or a buyer for an overseas government or company. (The information sources listed in Chapter VIII can help you get in touch with export buyers). Here your sale will be just another domestic transaction, with payment made in the United States and without the need for you to worry about any of the details of export: packing, shipping, documentation, marketing, and other factors.

There are several advantages in selling to a buyer for export; you do not have to develop any export expertise of your own, nor invest in export staff, nor export promotion; your credit risk is the same as for any other domestic sale and the orders generally come to you. The disadvantages are obvious; your "export" sales are dependent upon what the export buyer decides to make them, you have no direct contact with the overseas customer and cannot promote continued, long-range business. The buyer can shop around and find another supplier and then you lose these additional sales. If you go this route, you are not really in the export business at all, but you may develop some extra sales on a short term basis.

You can become more active in export and still let someone else do it for you, by using the services of a Combination Export Manager. A CEM as he is called, may be a one-man operation or a large company. The CEM acts as the export department for a number of non-competing suppliers (often in a given field). He handles all the details of exporting, promotes your product abroad and may (or may not, depending upon your agreement) assume all credit risks. He may operate on a world-wide basis, or in a given area, or in a set number of countries. He may have branch offices abroad, or his own network of distributors. In some cases, the CEM will handle your exports for a retainer plus a commission on sales, in other cases he may work on a straight commission basis. (You can explore the possibilities of working through a CEM by talking with some of the information sources listed in Chapter VIII, or by making a direct contact with several CEM's through the CEM associations that are listed in the same chapter.)

The advantages offered by the CEM are similar to those given for sales to an export buyer, but the business potential is generally larger. However, you may have to become more familiar with the details of export, such as export packing, export marking and product tailoring, as the CEM is, in effect, an extension of your own company and will expect you to move your product direct to port for shipment in accordance with his instructions. This means that your shipping department will have to be prepared to handle the necessary export packing and marking and you will have to furnish the CEM with quotations the way he needs them (perhaps figuring out export weights in the metric system and furnishing the export cube of the item). You may also have to provide him with sales promotion literature and catalogs in various languages—at your expense.

There are disadvantages to the CEM approach to export, the main one being that although the CEM will do more promoting of your product than will the Export Buyer, the CEM is generally handling a number of other products for other companies at the same time and may not be willing, or able, to give your product all the attention you'd like to see it get. Again, as in the case of the export buyer, you generally do not have direct contact with the customer abroad and cannot develop long-range business. Despite these limitations, a good many United States companies have been using CEM's for long periods of time and are happy with the results. Others use CEM's in specific markets to augment their direct exports when they are not prepared to export on a world-wide basis (or have some other good reason).

There is still another version of this indirect method of exporting. This is referred to as the piggyback or "Mother Hen" approach. Under this method, an exporting manufacturer agrees to handle exports for a non-competing supplier (generally of an allied line) using his own export staff, know-how and connections.

Compile a list of the pros and cons on why you should (or should not) use a C.E.M. (Combination Export Manager).

PRO	CON

The direct approach to export has three variations. You can set up your own built-in export department, or organize a separate export division, or create a subsidiary company to handle your international activities. Each of these involves expense and staff and calls for a greater involvement and commitment than using the indirect approach. However, the rewards can be well worth the additional expense and effort.

The built-in export department usually starts off as a one-man operation. Frequently a company will assign the responsibility for developing exports to someone already on the staff. In some instances, an experienced export executive might be hired right at the beginning, if management has an understanding of the potential that exists for its products in world markets. Regardless of which of these two choices is made, the company that is serious about wanting to develop exports must be prepared to give the person selected to manage exports its full support. As this person will have to busy himself with export correspondence, finding distributors, learning how to work with export service organizations, providing the factory with the information and guidance it needs and educating all of the other departments to the export routine, he will only be able to perform effectively if he has the support and assistance he needs. Even though this may start off as a one-man show, it will not be too long until a full time secretary will be needed and then perhaps an assistant to handle things when the number one man (or woman— and there are a ·number of successful female exporters handling both consumer and industrial lines) is away from his office on business.

The success achieved by the built-in export department is clearly predicated upon the willing cooperation of management and the personnel of the other departments who have to back up the export manager. This means that as overseas sales grow, the entire company will have to become export-conscious and give export the attention it needs and deserves.

Suppose you were to set up your own built-in export department, do you have someone who could take on the added duties of export, or would you have to hire an experienced export manager? Draw up a rough table of organization for such a department and take a guess at costs—then talk this over with some of the experts.

_____

_____

_____

_____

As the company's export business expands, it may decide to move into the next stage—that of setting up a separate export department. Here the export manager becomes responsible for all the export activities and has his own personnel handling all the operations connected with export—sales, promotion, credit and shipping. The separate export department may continue to work from the company headquarters, or in the case of an inland company, may be moved to a port city.

The decision to establish a separate international company, or subsidiary, is generally determined by a considerable increase in volume and by tax or legal considerations. When a company reaches this stage in its international business, it may be ready for overseas manufacture through licensing or joint ventures. However, by this time, it should have developed considerable export know-how and sophistication—but before we get too involved in these more advanced export or international business techniques, it would be well to consider some of the more basic aspects of developing overseas sales.

With someone assigned to handle exports, a company can proceed to develop its international trade. Initial orders, or at least correspondence, may have already been received from abroad. Sometimes this unsolicited business comes about because an overseas businessman visiting the United States has seen the product or an advertisement for it in a domestic magazine, and inquires about it upon his return home. In other cases, a United States government source may have given the name of the company to a prospective buyer as a likely supplier. (Foreign businessmen and government procurement agencies came to the United States Department of Commerce in 1966 with more than 15,000 requests for help in finding suppliers of American-made products.) Perhaps the company itself has done some sales promotion work of its own (more on this in the next chapter). Regardless of how the initial inquiry develops, it should not be overlooked and steps should be taken to handle it properly.

Taking the simplest case, let's assume that a letter arrives at the company headquarters asking for information on a product, its cost and possible delivery date. Frequently this letter may arrive in a foreign language and will have to be translated. Once we know what the request is for, we can proceed to supply the information. However, we now find that we have to learn how to quote so the overseas buyer will be able to compare our price with that of other suppliers. This means that we have to understand how we arrive at an export quotation. To the experienced exporter, the proper export price is one that covers the cost of manufacture, profit, and cost of export (export department expense, credit or financing charges if any, packing, insurance and shipping charges). It should not include any purely domestic expenses, otherwise the price may be too high to be realistic.

In addition to price information, the quotation should spell out clearly which of the transportation and insurance charges are included. Bear in mind that the buyer overseas may find it difficult to figure out what the transportation charges will be if the quotation is F.O.B. (Free on Board) factory. It is generally considered better to quote on a C.I.F. (Cost, Insurance and Freight) basis to the overseas port. Then the buyer can determine what the inland freight in his own country will be. A C.I.F. quotation enables you to have greater control over the shipment until it reaches the buyer's country, but do not assume that this should be your standard quote—in some countries, government regulations may not permit insurance to be covered in the United States. (You can get plenty of help in determining how to quote from the service organizations and the experts listed in Chapter VIII.)

While we are on this subject of export price quotations, it is worth noting that there is a difference between the definitions of these terms as used in the United States and in other countries. In the United States the basic authority on these quotations is a list drawn up and approved by several industry associations, known as the "Revised American Foreign Trade Definitions—1941." A similar compilation of trade definitions called "Incoterms, 1953," is sponsored by the International Chamber of Commerce. It reflects certain European usage and understanding of trade terms and does differ somewhat from the American list. Most American exporters specify that their terms are subject to the "Revised American Foreign Trade Definitions—1941" and make certain their customers abroad understand and agree to these definitions of responsibility. The important thing to remember is that both seller and buyer must know exactly what the terms mean and cover and who is responsible for what. It would be unwise to assume that the overseas customer understands what you mean—it would be advisable to spell out clearly all points so that no misunderstanding can arise. (The full listing of the "Revised American Foreign Trade Definitions—1941" appears in the back of this book.

Besides coming up with the export price quotation, you have to make certain that you give the prospective buyer complete information on the product, explaining when necessary any and all technical details that might not be apparent to someone unfamiliar with the product. You will have to find out from the customer abroad what import regulations may apply to your product and how you can live up to them. In some countries you may have to supply labels in the local language, or have your product go through a government testing office. An import license may be needed and you will have to make certain the buyer has one before shipping (otherwise your product may be confiscated when it arrives). Your product may require a United States export license and you will have to check with the United States Department of Commerce to find out about this. You will have to commit yourself to a firm shipping date and will need the proper information from a freight forwarder or transportation company. In many cases you will have to prepare certain documents for the use of the overseas country's officials in the United States—here again, a freight forwarder can be very helpful. Product tailoring may be required and you will have to rely on the overseas buyer or agent, to give you this information.

In addition to providing all of the information requested as promptly as you can (remember the time lag overseas and send it by airmail) and supplying it in the proper language if possible, you should immediately, or perhaps even before you answer, learn all you can about the prospective buyer. You can draw a Dun and Bradstreet International Credit Report, or check with your bank, or the Department of Commerce. You can also ask the buyer to submit his bank references and the names of other United States suppliers so you can check with them. You should explore the extension of credit thoroughly with your banker.

There are several ways in which you can get payment for export sales and the method of payment will frequently depend on both the country and the customer. The most obvious method of payment is cash in advance, or on shipment. Quite a bit of international trade, however, involves credit and once a company gets to know enough about export and overseas customers, the extension of credit becomes routine. One of the frequently used payment methods is the letter of credit whereby a bank overseas upon receipt of the customer's payment or through extending him credit, issues a letter of credit in favor of the seller through a United States bank which pays when certain conditions have been met by the seller. Letters of credit have several variations and your banker can guide you on their use. In addition to letters of credit, another instrument of payment is the draft—which is basically a written order to pay—again after certain conditions have been met. However there are different kinds of drafts— sight, time and date, and you should consult your banker on them. Overseas sales are also made on consignment and on open account. Most successful exporters are flexible in their credit policies and will vary their terms to meet market conditions.

Once you have determined your quotation and are satisfied with the information obtained on the overseas buyer, you can then proceed to handle whatever business may develop.

1549410

CHAPTER 4

Promoting Export Sales

Export Sales Promotion can take many forms. A company
with no previous international experience can try out its
products in overseas markets with a minimum of expense
by taking advantage of various United States government
programs. One of these enables a company to exhibit its
products in certain overseas countries. There are three
variations to this exhibit program: Trade Centers, Sample
Display Centers and Trade Exhibits.

Trade Centers are permanent exhibition showrooms
maintained in eight overseas cities (London, Frankfurt,
Milan, Paris, Tokyo, Stockholm, Sydney and Bangkok)
where groups of related United States products are displayed for specified periods. These displays are changed
frequently allowing a wide range of American products to

be shown. The Trade Centers are staffed by United States officials who help exhibitors find agents, distributors and buyers for the different products displayed.

Most times the results of exhibiting at a Trade Center are highly productive. Sometimes they can be a bit unusual. One Texas company making a machine to sort peanuts electronically took part in a Tokyo Center show. They figured that the electronic peanut sorter, although a relatively expensive item, might find a few buyers in Japan because the Japanese are fond of baseball, and peanuts and baseball go together. One of the visitors to the show owned a large pearl company and upon seeing the peanut sorter in action, wondered if it would work with pearls. It did, and the sale was made and several others were soon lined up.

Not only do large companies benefit from participation in these Trade Center shows, but so do small companies. A manufacturer of cotton potholders in Memphis, Tennessee, (with only eight employees) exhibited his wares at a London show. As a result he has developed an overseas business to the point where 20% of his production is now being exported.

Sample Display Centers are maintained at various United States embassies. At these Display Centers, United States companies can show samples of their products (with descriptive literature) without charge.

Trade Exhibits are sponsored by the United States Department of Commerce at many of the international trade fairs held each year. The Department arranges for exhibit space at the fair and invites suppliers of specific products to exhibit. (More details on all of these available from the Department of Commerce offices.)

38

List the address of the United States Department of Commerce office closest to you and any other information sources that can help you (see Chapter VIII).

_____

_____

_____

_____

_____

_____

_____

In addition to these three exhibit facilities offered by the government, each involving the actual display of the product, there is another way to acquaint overseas prospects with a company and its product. There are a number of government-sponsored trade missions that go abroad each year. These missions take with them various business proposals—offers to sell, buy or enter into a commercial relationship—from United States companies. Any reputable company can submit a business proposal (no charge) to the Department of Commerce in advance of one of these missions. Mission members meet with businessmen, local government and United States officials in the country and actively promote the business of the companies who have submitted proposals (they also bring back similar proposals from businessmen in the overseas country). A similar business proposal service is offered at United States business information centers maintained at selected international trade fairs.

The United States government is not the only one helping companies sell in world markets. A number of the transportation companies (such as Pan American, TWA and Farrell Lines) have set up their own trade development departments and offer a variety of services to the company seeking to build sales abroad. Some will bring buyer and seller together through personal contact, others publish bulletins and will include listings without charge. There are private exhibitions of United States products held in certain markets at different times of the year and from time to time, private trade missions, often on a state or industry basis, go abroad. (The information sources covered in Chapter VIII can supply more details on these.)

Besides using the exhibit possibilities and the business proposals, a company can do quite a bit on its own to build its international business. The easiest way to make contact with likely buyers overseas is to study the vast number of trade leads that are issued regularly throughout the country and select appropriate prospects. These trade leads, specific inquiries from overseas businessmen to buy, sell or represent, can be found in many places. The United States Department of Commerce magazine, International Commerce, carries them weekly; the various trade associations issue them; the state trade promotion offices—such as New York State's International Commerce Department—put them out; so do the trade promotion offices of the transportation companies. From these leads, a company can build its own direct mail list for continuous sales promotion work.

Direct mail offers numerous possibilities to a company. It can introduce a product to a market, make sales, and uncover agents or representatives. In addition to building a direct mail list from trade leads, a company can make use of trade directories (such as the Dun and Bradstreet International Market Guides) and of the Department of Commerce trade lists to compile its prospect file.

Such a file or list of prospects can be as long or as short as the company wants it to be. It can be a simple name and address list by country, or it can be more elaborate with each entry showing credit information, financial standing, area covered, and other representations as desired. Regardless of what kind of information is covered in such a prospect file, it should be used on a continuous basis to produce results. A company may decide to do its own direct mail promotion or to use the services of one of the international sales promotion specialists; either way, the direct mail program should be carefully planned. Since most overseas mail should go by air, the cost factor will have to be considered and the direct mail material should be designed to be lightweight, but still able to tell the complete story. If catalogs are being sent, make certain you know what the regulations are for the country to which they are going—in some cases there may be duty on them. If you plan to design a single mailing piece for a number of countries, consider the use of a multi-language mailing piece (remember the point covered on this in Chapter II).

Take a look at your present direct mail material and consider what you would have to do to use this material abroad.

_____

_____

_____

_____

While direct mail is the most often used method of promoting overseas sales, it is not the only way; advertising is employed effectively by many companies. There are quite a few United States-based publications that circulate in overseas markets and carry ads. In addition, a number of overseas newspapers, magazines, radio and TV stations have representatives in the United States. Both the United States and the overseas media representatives can be extremely helpful in providing a company with market information and advertising advice. When it comes to advertising, bear in mind that the right press media may simply not exist in a given country and you may have to settle for running your technical ads in a consumer paper. TV may be the best and lowest cost medium for greatest results in one country, while in another it may not be available to enough people. In quite a few markets, radio is still the best way to reach the most prospects. Movie advertising is used successfully in some countries and is worth looking into. Use of expensive printed material in a largely illiterate nation can be a waste unless it is highly pictorial. There are a number of experts who can guide you on the proper advertising for your product. Quite a few United States advertising agencies are well posted on international markets, many having their own offices abroad. The International Advertising Association (see Chapter VIII) can be helpful in making contact with agencies handling overseas advertising for American companies.

When you do decide to advertise abroad, make certain you have a good idea of what to do and how to do it. Remember that advertising overseas is not the same as in the United States. You have to accept the fact that in all probability neither your product nor your company are known by your prospects. You may have to spend advertising dollars to develop company identity and acceptance—stressing reliability and how long you have been in business—before you get down to the actual sales pitch. You will want to make sure your advertising provides sufficient information to enable your prospect to make a valid judgment. This means that if yours is a technical product you provide data in keeping with market requirements. Weights and measurements will probably have to be in the metric system; other specifications that may be different from what is standard in the United States will have to be spelled out in terms that the prospect can understand. Don't take anything for granted either! The Department of Commerce points out that there can even be a difference in the size of an inch. A United States businessman visiting a furniture factory in Yugoslavia found workmen using a tape measure marked off in "Vienna inches," 24 of which equal 25 United States inches. Upon checking, the Department learned that there are a number of other unofficial "inches" of varying lengths used in Europe.

Bear in mind, also, that overseas prospects may be motivated to buy for vastly different reasons than are your domestic customers. The labor-saving benefits of certain equipment will not have the same appeal in a country where labor is cheap and plentiful as it would in the domestic market and other benefits will have to be played up. You should check this out carefully with the people who know the market before going ahead with your advertising program.

Don't overlook the role of public relations and publicity in your international sales promotion work. A public relations program, if used properly, can be an effective way to pre-condition a market so that your prospects become familiar with your product, its use and your company name. Even the simplest new product release sent to the international publications, or to overseas media can turn up prospects. While your own company public relations or promotion man can soon learn how to publicize your product overseas, there are a number of international public relations companies in the United States who can be called upon for help.

If you wanted to start promoting overseas sales tomorrow, what would be your first step? How much would it cost? How would you proceed?

Overseas sales promotion, just like domestic, is a never-ending job and it will pay you to learn all you can about the proper use of direct mail, advertising, trade shows and public relations overseas.

CHAPTER 5

Overseas Travel

When it comes to promoting exports, one of the most productive ways can be the visit to the market. While overseas travel at first glance may seem expensive, most successful exporters consider it a must. Do not rush off on a trip, however, without careful planning so that you know where to go and whom to see. (This also means paying close attention to the points covered in Chapter II). While your travel agent can make all the necessary arrangements for your trip—line up hotel reservations and connecting flights (most business travelers go by air)—he cannot make the business contacts that you will need (certain airlines may be helpful here).

There are sources you can turn to for such help. The United States Department of Commerce, through its Field Offices, can make arrangements whereby United States Foreign Service officers in the cities to be visited are alerted concerning the details and objectives of your trip. They, if given sufficient advance notice, can line up visits with likely prospects and provide current, on-the-spot information and advice. So one of the first things to do when going abroad is to check in with Commerce.

In addition to the help waiting for you at the Department of Commerce, you can also make contacts through other sources in the United States, such as local American Chambers of Commerce, Dun and Bradstreet offices, your bank and transportation contacts. The United States representatives of overseas governments, as well as the foreign chambers in this country, can also supply leads and advice for business travelers. The important thing is to make certain you have lined up your schedule of visits before you take off for overseas markets; otherwise, you can waste a great deal of time when you get there. It's a good idea to have current credit information on all the companies with which you expect to meet.

If you were to plan a trip abroad, which markets would you want to visit? Whom would you call upon? How would you make your contacts? Take a few minutes to lay out a plan of action.

Be realistic in your travel planning—a trip of more than three weeks can be too long and tiring to be really productive. It would be better to plan on several trips during the year rather than to attempt to cover too many markets at once. If you do try to cover a number of them, you will probably not spend enough time in any one of them to be effective. Don't forget that your actual working time in the market will be restricted by the travel time required to get from one to another and the fact that you'll not be operating at peak efficiency after a lengthy trip and should take some time out to rest up. Weekends will also cut into your time and you should check on the holidays in the countries you are going to visit, or you may find yourself unable to do any business if you arrive during a lengthy holiday.

Draw up a checklist of things to do and what to take, well in advance of your departure date. Make sure you have an up-to-date passport, vaccination, necessary inoculations, travelers' checks (and a supply of one dollar bills and perhaps some local currency for immediate use at airports). Study the travel information available from the airlines and the tourist offices of the respective countries, so you will know what to wear and how much to take in the way of baggage. Make certain to confirm your reservation about 24 hours before departure and do this at each stop.

Draw up a checklist of things to do and of what to take on your trip.

1. _____

_____

2. _____

_____

_____

3. _____

_____

_____

4. _____

_____

_____

5. _____

_____

Once you arrive at your destination and have checked into your hotel, review your objectives. If you expect to meet with several prospective agents or distributors and sign one up, do not rush off to make a number of calls with little knowledge of the market, local business customs and trade practices. Check with the local United States government officials, the chamber of commerce, or any other business authorities that you can find, to learn how business is done in the market and who are the most likely prospects for you to see. When you have drawn up a list, do not attempt to make too many calls in a single day. You will have to remember that in many countries, people take a more leisurely approach to business and you may have to spend more time on each call than you'd expect. Always remember that customs differ overseas and while some people will accept them, others resent our so-called "high pressure" methods of doing business. Quite often good international business relationships mean good personal relationships and it is well to go slowly in your initial meetinge with people in other countries. Find out how people act and react in the country so that you can develop a smooth working relationship. This does not mean "going native," but it does mean that you do everything possible to recognize and respect the customs of the people you meet and the country you visit. In some countries the altitude or temperature may take some getting-used-to and you may find it wise to move at a slower pace.

With a little advance planning it may be possible to time your visit to coincide with a trade fair, or an exhibition being held at a United States trade center and you can combine your prospect work with a visit to the show. By spending an extra day or two in the country you can get a better feel of the market, size up the competition and perhaps re-think your plans for your sales development and market cultivation work.

What would be the best time of the year for your visit? How long could you afford to spend in each market?

_____

_____

_____

_____

_____

_____

In addition to attending to the various details outlined here, before taking off on your trip—as a matter of fact, quite a few weeks before—it would be advisable to send off sales literature and possibly samples, to your attention, care of the hotels where you plan to stay. In this way, you will not be burdened with carrying these items on your trip and will be sure to have an adequate supply when you go out into the marketplace. It's a good idea to have an ample supply of business cards with you as in some countries, Japan for example, you exchange them with each businessman you meet—sometimes this means eight or ten in a given meeting. A sample collection of sales literature should be sent on to each prospective agent or distributor at the time you notify him of your expected arrival date in his country.

You will want to make certain that your home office has a copy of your itinerary and that your secretary or assistant knows where and how to reach you at any given time. It's also a good idea to mail back any material you may gather in a particular country before moving on, rather than to try to carry it all with you. Not only will this relieve you of extra weight in your baggage, but it may prevent you from running into trouble with customs in the next country you visit.

CHAPTER 6

Selecting Agents and Distributors

The company seeking to build sales abroad will have to depend for a great deal of its success upon the agents or distributors it selects. (An agent or representative makes sales on a commission basis, a distributor buys and sells —and generally stocks and services—for his own account). Occasionally some United States firms have tied themselves up with agents or distributors solely on the strength of a few letters. They do not know enough about the man (or company), his ability, reputation, financial position, and sometimes after a period of inactivity decide that the market is no good, or that they shouldn't bother with export after all. This is why a visit to the market can be so important—it provides an opportunity to get to meet and know the prospective agent or distributor before you make any agreement.

What should you look for in an agent or distributor? First of all, you will want someone who is honest and who enjoys a favorable reputation (draw a credit report). Next, you want someone who can and will work to build business—some agents or distributors may have gotten too "fat and lazy" to be really productive, but will still take on your line simply to cash in on any business that may come in without effort. You should be looking for someone who can cover the market properly, has the sales organization (and service facilities if needed), has the staff and financial ability to carry sufficient stock and replacement parts. You'll also want to make certain that your product line is in harmony with the others he may be handling and that he doesn't represent any competitors.

Consider the things you'd look for in an agent or distributor. How large an operation should he have? How much stock should he carry? Would he need to have service facilities?

_____

_____

_____

_____

On your visit to the market you should make it a point to see the prospective agent or distributor's place of business and find out what kind of a setup he has. You should talk with some of his sales people and find out how well trained they are and whether or not they will be able to do the job. If possible, find out who his other principals are and try to learn about his performance from them. In addition, see if you can determine how well posted he is on long term developments in his field and his country. Find out if he is aware of his country's development programs and has the right contacts so that you do not miss out on any potential business.

Bear in mind that good salesmen are not as easy to come by in many countries as they are in the United States and that quite often training of both sales and service people is a "must." A few hours spent with a prospective distributor's sales people can be well worth while and will enable you to find out how much and what kind of training may be needed. Some United States companies have found it very productive to bring overseas sales and service people to the United States for training at the factory or head office. Some have developed a training program that is put on in the overseas market. In addition to these specific training programs, a number of exporters will set up periodic sales meetings in a centrally located city and then bring together their overseas representatives for a sales conference. For a company with worldwide coverage, this could mean two or three different area meetings, say one for Europe and one for Latin America and Asia.

Once you have settled upon the right man (or company), then what? Some exporters will do business on the strength of a handshake, others will settle for a simple letter from each party. Some insist upon a formal agreement. Whichever method you decide to use is up to you, but it is well to make certain your agreement covers a set period of time; that it spells out responsibilities clearly; that it documents area to be covered and that the agent or distributor will not handle competing products. It's generally considered a good idea to arrange a trial period of less than a year so that both parties will have a chance to find out how they will work together and whether the arrangement will be mutually profitable. Remember that you have to exercise care in making these arrangements because some countries have regulations or trade practices under which the agent or distributor will have long term compensation rights based on the goodwill he may have developed even after you have decided to terminate the arrangement. It's a good idea to check this out with an attorney—preferably one familiar with international trade before signing anything. Besides making the right agreement, you should pay attention to such things as local advertising in the market and perhaps work out a joint program, or at least state what your policy will be.

What kind of agreement would be best for you? What points should it cover? For how long? If you can, outline your requirements—if not, draw up a list of points to check on.

1. _____

_____

2. _____

_____

3. _____

_____

4. _____

_____

5. _____

_____

Since the distributor or agent can perform well only if you do—make plans to keep in close contact with him. Write often and send all sales literature, new product information, training material for use by his people and all promotional material issued by your company (even the house organ so he begins to think of himself as part of the family). Draw up realistic marketing plans in cooperation with him and review them periodically. Have a planned schedule of visits to the market and try to follow it. Some experienced exporters visit their overseas representatives at least once every other year and have them make visits to the United States in between.

There are many things that can be done to build a profitable, lasting relationship with your overseas agents or distributors (in some cases you may want to use an agent in one market and a distributor in another, depending upon business potential). Don't give an overseas represetative too big an area to cover—such as Central America or Europe unless you are sure he can handle it. Make sure you answer correspondence promptly and ship on time. See to it that he is informed if for any reason delays are to be expected. Handle the processing of all payments as quickly as possible. Encourage his participation in trade shows—perhaps on a cooperative basis. Always remember that he is a long way from headquarters and needs all the support and encouragement that you can give him.

CHAPTER 7

Export Service Organizations

Once a company becomes active in export, it soon learns that there are a number of service organizations ready, able and willing to help it with the different steps involved in selling, shipping and getting paid for its goods. While some exporting companies may make more use of a different combination of these organizations, in general, the newcomer would probably come in contact with them in the following order:

1. BANKER. A banker should be able to provide help with a company's basic deliberations on export, offer guidance on credit, financing and the handling of documents. He may also be able to provide assistance in making contacts overseas. Even a number of the smaller, domestic United States banks have become familiar with export and through their correspondent banks, which are more active in international trade, can obtain information and supply answers to export questions.

2. FREIGHT FORWARDER. The forwarder will handle all the details involved in moving the goods to the cus-

tomer. He will prepare the necessary papers, arrange for transportation, customs clearance, marine insurance and forward banking collection papers and instructions.

3. EXPORT PACKER. Quite a number of exporters use the services of independent export packers who are equipped to do a thorough job of packing goods for export. Generally located at portside, the export packing company can receive goods unpacked or in domestic cartons and do the necessary export packing to assure safe arrival overseas.

4. TRANSPORTATION COMPANIES. Rail, truck, air and steamship companies all have their role in export and most have experienced export representatives who are willing to visit a prospective exporter and provide a great deal of assistance on trade practices as well as make arrangements for the movement of goods. (Frequently a freight forwarder is employed to handle these transportation arrangements, but some companies with their own traffic departments work direct.)

5. DUN & BRADSTREET. D&B provides credit reports on overseas companies; has available International Market Guides for Latin America and Europe and various reference and credit directories for other countries; can do certain market research work and handle collections. D&B publishes *Exporters' Encyclopaedia,* a basic handbook for exporters, and an international business magazine *Business Abroad* is published by the Rueben H. Donnelley Corporation, a member of the Dun & Bradstreet Group.

6. MARINE INSURANCE BROKERS. Provide advice and

the necessary insurance to cover export cargo and can be helpful in settling claims.

7. FOREIGN CREDIT INSURANCE ASSOCIATION. FCIA insures trade credits granted by United States exporters to responsible buyers in all free world markets. The risks covered by FCIA are: (a) commercial credit, i.e. insolvency and protracted payment default, and (b) political risks, i.e. exchange transfer delay, war, revolution, expropriation and other causes of loss arising principally from government action and beyond the control of buyer or seller.

8. UNITED STATES PORTS. Most United States ports have developed their own trade promotion departments and are in a position to help the shipper with a considerable amount of information and advice. Many ports have offices or traveling representatives covering different parts of the country—some have offices abroad.

9. INTERNATIONAL ADVERTISING AND PUBLIC RELATIONS AGENCIES. With the growth of United States trade a number of advertising and public relations agencies are devoting more time and attention to international business. They can offer many services to the newcomer (and experienced exporter) on overseas markets and sales promotion.

10. CONSULTANTS. There are a number of experienced international business consultants who can provide a variety of export help and guidance. Some of these are individuals, others have staffs of varying size. Some are expert in certain areas of export or in certain world markets. Their know-how can often be worth quite a bit more than their fee.

CHAPTER 8

Information Sources/Services

There are many sources a company can turn to for help in developing an export business. These range from government offices to private industry sources and from offices located in the United States to offices abroad.

The United States Department of Commerce is the principal agency concerned with our overseas business. It provides a wide range of know-how and services through its 42 Field Offices (see list) and in Washington. Within the Department of Commerce, the Bureau of International Commerce is the primary office responsible for the development and promotion of United States trade abroad. Under the National Export Expansion Program, the Department of Commerce has set up Regional Export Expansion Councils (REEC) across the United States. Operating out of the 42 Field Offices, these Councils are composed of experienced international trade authorities who work with chambers of commerce, trade associations, export service organizations and schools to arrange courses, provide speakers and set up trade conferences. In addition, REEC members are available for private consultations with prospective exporters. They may be contacted through any of the United States Department of Commerce Field Offices.

Other United States Government Agencies, such as the State Department (principally the Agency for International Development—AID—which can provide direct business leads through its Office of Small Business); the Department of Agriculture and the Export-Import Bank, also offer services and information to exporters.

The United Nations, through its various agencies (World Health Organization, Food and Agricultural Organization, United Nations Development Program) compiles and disseminates a wealth of information of value to companies seeking to develop overseas sales. Some of these agencies do their own buying for various programs.

Many of the state governments maintain their own trade promotion offices which will provide general information and trade leads; many sponsor trade missions.

Industry shares information through numerous trade associations such as the National Foreign Trade Council, the International Executives Association, The International Trade Club of Chicago, The World Trade Club of New York and others located in many cities. A number of local Chambers of Commerce have international departments. While most of these are membership organizations, the newcomer will be able to meet staff members and will frequently find valuable assistance available through them.

In addition to these general trade associations, there are a number of specific industry groups that one can turn to, such as the American Institute of Merchant Shipping or the International Advertising Association and the National Customs Brokers and Freight Forwarders Association and others.

There are a number of places that can be utilized to learn more about these various information sources—the local telephone book, Department of Commerce Field Office, public library and various publications. One reference source, *Exporters' Encyclopaedia,* contains information on all of them. Available from Dun and Bradstreet, the Encyclopaedia has been used effectively for more than 60 years by both experienced exporters and newcomers to the export field.

Following are the names and addresses of many of the information sources covered in this chapter:

United States Department of Commerce, Bureau of International Commerce, Washington, D. C. 20230.

U.S. Department of Commerce—Field Offices:

Albuquerque, N. Mex., 87101, U. S. Courthouse. Area Code 505, 843-2386.

Anchorage, Alaska, 99501, 412 Hill Bldg., 632 Sixth Ave. Area Code 907, 272-6531.

Atlanta, Ga., 30303, 4th Floor Home Savings Bldg., 75 Forsyth St., N.W. Area Code 404, 526-6000.

Baltimore, Md., 21202, 305 U.S. Customhouse, Gay and Lombard Sts. Area Code 301, 962-3560.

Birmingham, Ala., 35205, Suite 200-201, 908 S. 20th St. Area Code 205, 325-3327.

Boston, Mass., 02203, Room 510, John Fitzgerald Kennedy Federal Bldg. Area Code 617, 223-2312.

Buffalo, N. Y., 14203, 504 Federal Bldg., 117 Ellicott St. Area Code 716, 842-3208.

Charleston, S. C., 29403, Federal Bldg., Suite 631, 334 Meeting St. Area Code 803, 577-4171.

Charleston, W. Va., 25301, 3000 New Federal Office Bldg., 500 Quarrier St. Area Code 304, 343-6181 Ext. 375 and 376.

Cheyenne, Wyo., 82001, 6022 Federal Bldg., 2120 Capitol Ave. Area Code 307, 634-5920.

Chicago, Ill., 60604, 1486 New Federal Bldg., 219 S. Dearborn St. Area Code 312, 353-4400.

Cincinnati, Ohio, 45202, 8028 Federal Office Bldg., 550 Main St. Area Code 513, 684-2944.

Cleveland, Ohio, 44114, Room 600, 666 Euclid Ave. Area Code 216, 522-4750.

Dallas, Tex., 75202, Room 1200, 1114 Commerce St. Area Code 214, 749-3287.

Denver, Colo., 80202, 16419 Federal Bldg., 20th and Stout Sts. Area Code 303, 297-3246.

Des Moines, Iowa, 50309, 609 Federal Bldg., 210 Walnut St. Area Code 515, 284-4222.

Detroit, Mich., 48226, 445 Federal Bldg. Area Code 313, 226-6088.

Greensboro, N. C., 27402, 258 Federal Bldg., W. Market St. P.O. Box 1950. Area Code 919, 275-9111.

Hartford, Conn., 06103, Room 610-B, Federal Office Bldg., 450 Main St. Area Code 203, 244-3530.

Honolulu, Hawaii, 96813, 286 Alexander Young Bldg., 1015 Bishop St. Area Code 808, 546-5977.

Houston, Tex., 77002, 5102 Federal Bldg., 515 Rusk Ave. Area Code 713, 226-4231.

Jacksonville, Fla., 32202, P.O. Box 35087, 400 W. Bay St. Area Code 904, 791-2796.

Kansas City, Mo., 64106, Room 1840, 601 E. 12th St. Area Code 816, 374-3141.

Los Angeles, Calif., 90024, 11th Floor, Federal Bldg., 11000 Wilshire Blvd. Area Code 213, 824-7591.

Memphis, Tenn., 38103, 710 First American Bank Bldg., 147 Jefferson Ave. Area Code 901, 534-3214.

Miami, Fla., 33130, Rm. 821, City National Bank Bldg., 25 W. Flagler St. Area Code 305, 350-5267.

Milwaukee, Wis., 53203, Straus Bldg., 238 W. Wisconsin Ave. Area Code 414, 272-8600.

Minneapolis, Minn., 55401, 306 Federal Bldg., 110 S. Fourth St. Area Code 612, 725-2133.

New Orleans, La., 70130, 909 Federal Office Bldg., S., 610 South St. Area Code 504, 527-6546.

New York, N. Y., 10007, 41st Floor, Federal Office Bldg., 26 Federal Plaza, Foley Sq. Area Code 212, 264-0634.

Philadelphia, Pa., 19107, Jefferson Bldg., 1015 Chestnut St. Area Code 215, 597-2850.

Phoenix, Ariz., 85025, 5413 New Federal Bldg., 230 N. First Ave. Area Code 602, 261-3285.

Pittsburgh, Pa., 15222, 2201 Federal Bldg., 1000 Liberty Ave. Area Code 412, 644-2850.

Portland, Ore., 97204, 217 Old U.S. Courthouse, 520 S.W. Morrison St. Area Code 503, 226-3361.

Reno, Nev., 89502, 2028 Federal Bldg., 300 Booth St. Area Code 702, 784-5203.

Richmond, Va., 23240, 2105 Federal Bldg., 400 N. 8th St. Area Code 703, 649-3611.

St. Louis, Mo., 63103, 2511 Federal Bldg., 1520 Market St. Area Code 314, 622-4243.

Salt Lake City, Utah, 84111, 3235 Federal Bldg., 125 S. State St. Area Code 801, 524-5116.

San Francisco, Calif., 94102, Federal Bldg., Box 36013, 450 Golden Gate Ave. Area Code 415, 556-5864.

San Juan, P.R., 00902, Room 100, Post Office Bldg. Phone 723-4640.

Savannah, Ga., 31402, 235 U.S. Courthouse and Post Office Bldg., 125-29 Bull St. Area Code 912, 232-4321.

Seattle, Wash., 98104, 8021 Federal Office Bldg., 909 First Ave. Area Code 206, 583-5615.

New York State, Department of Commerce, 230 Park Ave., New York, N. Y. 10017.

National Customs Brokers & Forwarders Association, 26 Beaver St., New York, N. Y. 10004.

Foreign Credit Insurance Association, 250 Broadway, New York, N. Y. 10007.

International Advertising Association, 475 Fifth Ave., New York, N. Y. 10017.

National Foreign Trade Council, 10 Rockefeller Plaza, New York, N. Y. 10020.

International Executives Association, 432 Park Avenue South, New York, N. Y. 10016.

World Trade Club of New York, 99 Church St., New York, N. Y. 10007.

International Trade Club of Chicago, 140 S. Dearborn St., Chicago, Illinois 60603.

International Center of New England, 470 Atlantic Ave., Boston, Mass. 02210.

Export Manager's Association of San Francisco, 420 Montgomery St., San Francisco, Calif.

Export Managers' Club of New Orleans, International Trade Mart, New Orleans, La.

Associations of combination export management companies—CEM's:

National Association of Export Management Companies, 99 Church St., New York, N. Y. 10007.

Combination Export Managers Association of Connecticut, 222 Rimmon Road, North Haven, Conn. 06473.

Florida World Trade Association, P.O. Box 171, Miami International Airport, Miami, Fla. 33148.

Overseas Sales & Marketing Association of America, 1 East Wacker Drive, Chicago, Ill. 60601.

Michigan Association of Export Management Companies, 615 Griswold St., Detroit, Mich. 48226.

Council of Ohio Combination Export Managers, 690 Union Commerce Bldg., Cleveland, Ohio 44115.

CHAPTER 9

Revised American Foreign
Trade Definitions

FOREWORD

Since the issuance of *American Foreign Trade Definitions* in 1919, many changes in practice have occurred. The 1919 Definitions did much to clarify and simplify foreign trade practice, and received wide recognition and use by buyers and sellers throughout the world. At the Twenty-seventh National Foreign Trade Convention, 1940, further revision and clarification of these Definitions was urged as necessary to assist the foreign trader in the handling of his transactions.

The following *Revised American Foreign Trade Definitions*-1941 are recommended for general use by both exporters and importers. These revised definitions have no status at law unless there is specific legislation providing for them, or unless they are confirmed by court decisions. Hence, it is suggested that sellers and buyers agree to their acceptance as part of the contract of sale. These revised definitions will then become legally binding upon all parties.

In view of changes in practice and procedure since 1919, certain new responsibilities for sellers and buyers are included in these revised definitions. Also, in many instances, the old responsibilities are more clearly defined than in the 1919 Definitions, and the changes should be beneficial both to sellers and buyers. Widespread acceptance will lead to a greater standardization of foreign trade procedure, and to the avoidance of much misunderstanding.

Adoption by exporters and importers of these revised terms will impress on all parties concerned their respective responsibilities and rights.

Adopted July 30, 1941, by a Joint Committee representing the Chamber of Commerce of the United States of America, the National Council of American Importers, Inc., and the National Foreign Trade Council, Inc.

GENERAL NOTES OF CAUTION

1. As foreign trade definitions have been issued by organizations in various parts of the world, and as the courts of countries have interpreted these definitions in different ways, it is important that sellers and buyers agree that their contracts are subject to the *Revised American Foreign Trade Definitions*-1941 and that the various points listed are accepted by both parties.

2. In addition to the foreign trade terms listed herein, there are terms that are at times used, such as Free Harbor, C.I.F. & C. (Cost, Insurance, Freight, and Commission), C.I.F.C. & I. (Cost, Insurance, Freight, Commission, and Interest), C.I.F. Landed (Cost, Insurance, Freight, Landed), and others. None of these should be used unless there has first been a definite understanding as to the exact meaning thereof. It is unwise to attempt to interpret other terms in the light of the terms given herein. Hence, whenever possible, one of the terms defined herein should be used.

3. It is unwise to use abbreviations in quotations or in contracts which might be subject to misunderstanding.

4. When making quotations, the familiar terms "hundredweight" or "ton" should be avoided. A hundredweight can be 100 pounds of the short ton, or 112 pounds of the long ton. A ton can be a short ton of 2,000 pounds, or a metric ton of 2,204.6 pounds, or a long ton of 2,240 pounds. Hence, the type of hundredweight or ton should be clearly stated in quotations and in sales confirmations. Also, all terms referring to quantity, weight, volume, length, or surface should be clearly defined and agreed upon.

5. If inspection, or certificate of inspection, is required, it should be agreed, in advance, whether the cost thereof is for account of seller or buyer.

6. Unless otherwise agreed upon, all expenses are for the account of seller up to the point at which the buyer must handle the subsequent movement of goods.

7. There are a number of elements in a contract that do not fall within the scope of these foreign trade definitions. Hence, no mention of these is made herein. Seller and buyer should agree to these separately when negotiating contracts. This particularly applies to so-called "customary" practices.

DEFINITIONS OF QUOTATIONS
(I) Ex (Point of Origin)

"EX FACTORY," "EX MILL," "EX MINE," "EX PLANTATION," "EX WAREHOUSE," etc. (named point of Origin).

Under this term, the price quoted applies only at the point of origin, and the seller agrees to place the goods at the disposal of the buyer at the agreed place in the date or within the period fixed.

Under this quotation:

Seller must

1. Bear all costs and risks of the goods until such time as the buyer is obliged to take delivery thereof;

2. Render the buyer, at the buyer's request and expense, assistance in obtaining the documents issued in the country of origin, or of shipment, or of both, which the buyer may require either for purposes of exportation, or of importation at destination.

Buyer must

1. Take delivery of the goods as soon as they have been placed at his disposal at the agreed place on the date or within the period fixed;

2. Pay export taxes, or other fees or charges, if any, levied because of exportation;

3. Bear all costs and risks of the goods from the time when he is obligated to take delivery thereof;

4. Pay all costs and charges incurred in obtaining the documents issued in the country of origin, or of shipment, or of both, which may be required either for purposes of exportation, or of importation at destination.

(II) F.O.B. (Free on Board)

NOTE: *Seller and buyer should consider not only the defi-*

*nitions but also the "Comments on All F.O.B. Terms"
given at end of this section, in order to understand fully
their respective responsibilities and rights under the several classes of "F.O.B." terms.*

*(II-A) "F.O.B. (named inland carrier at named inland
point of departure)"**

Under this term, the price quoted applies only at inland shipping point, and the seller arranges for loading
of the goods on, or in, railway cars, trucks, lighters,
barges, aircraft, or other conveyance furnished for transportation.

Under this quotation:

Seller must

1. Place goods on, or in, conveyance, or deliver to inland
    carrier for loading;

2. Provide clean bill of lading or other transportation
    receipt, freight collect;

3. Be responsible for any loss or damage, or both, until
    goods have been placed in, or on, conveyance at load-
    ing point, and clean bill of lading or other transporta-
    tion receipt has been furnished by the carrier:

4. Render the buyer at the buyer's request and expense,
    assistance in obtaining the documents issued in the
    country of origin, or of shipment, or of both, which
    the buyer may require either for purposes of exporta-
    tion, or of importation at destination.

---

*See Note above and Comments on All F.O.B. Terms.

Buyer must

1. Be responsible for all movement of the goods from inland point of loading, and pay all transportation costs;

2. Pay export taxes, or other fees or charges, if any, levied because of exportation;

3. Be responsible for any loss or damage, or both, incurred after loading at named inland point of departure;

4. Pay all costs and charges incurred in obtaining the documents issued in the country of origin, or of shipment, or of both, which may be required either for purposes of exportation, or of importation at destination.

(II-B) "F.O.B." (named inland carrier at named inland point of departure) FREIGHT PREPAID TO (named point of exportation)"**

Under this term, the seller quotes a price including transportation charges to the named point of exportation and prepays freight to named point of exportation, without assuming responsibility for the goods after obtaining a clean bill of lading or other transportation receipt at named inland point of departure.

Under this quotation:

**See Note (II-A) and Comments on All F.O.B. Terms.

Seller must

1. Assume the seller's obligations as under II-A, except that under (2) he must provide clean bill of lading or other transportation receipt, freight prepaid to named point of exportation.

Buyer must

1. Assume the same buyer's obligations as under II-A, except that he does not pay freight from loading point to named point of exportation.

(II-C) "F.O.B." (named inland carrier at named inland point of departure) FREIGHT ALLOWED TO (named point)"**

Under this term, the seller quotes a price including the transportation charges to the named point, shipping freight collect and deducting the cost of transportation, without assuming responsibility for the goods after obtaining a clean bill of lading or other transportation receipt at named inland point of departure.

Under this quotation:

Seller must

1. Assume the same seller's obligations as under II-A, but deducts from his invoice the transportation cost to named point.

**See Note (II-A) and Comments on All F.O.B. Terms.

Buyer must

1. Assume the same buyer's obligations as under II-A, including payment of freight from inland loading point to named point, for which seller has made deduction.

(II-D) "F.O.B. (named inland carrier at named point of exportation)"**

Under this term, the seller quotes a price including the costs of transportation of the goods to named point of exportation, bearing any loss or damage, or both, incurred up to that point.

Under this quotation:

Seller must

1. Place goods on, or in, conveyance, or deliver to inland carrier for loading;

2. Provide clean bill of lading or other transportation receipt, paying all transportation costs from loading point to named point of exportation;

3. Be responsible for any loss or damage, or both, until goods have arrived in, or on, inland conveyance at the named point of exportation;

4. Render the buyer, at the buyer's request and expense, assistance in obtaining the documents issued in the country of origin, or of shipment, or of both, which

---

**See Note (II-A) and Comments on All F.O.B. Terms.

the buyer may require either for purposes of exportation, or of importation at destination.

Buyer must

1. Be responsible for all movement of the goods from
   inland conveyance at named point of exportation;

2. Pay export taxes, or other fees or charges, if any,
   levied because of exportation;

3. Be responsible for any loss or damage, or both, incurred after goods have arrived in, or on, inland conveyance at the named point of exportation;

4. Pay all costs and charges incurred in obtaining the
   documents issued in the country of origin, or of shipment, or of both, which may be required either for
   purposes of exportation, or of importation at destination.

*(II-E) "F.O.B." VESSEL (named port of shipment)"**

Under this term, the seller quotes a price covering all
expenses up to, and including, delivery of the goods upon
the overseas vessel provided by, or for, the buyer at the
named port of shipment.

Under this quotation:

Seller must

1. Pay all charges incurred in placing goods actually on
   board the vessel designated and provided by, or for,
   the buyer on the date or within the period fixed;

**See Note (II-A) and Comments on All F.O.B. Terms.

2. Provide clean ship's receipt or on-board bill of lading;

3. Be responsible for any loss or damage, or both, until goods have been placed on board the vessel on the date or within the period fixed;

4. Render the buyer, at the buyer's request and expense, assistance in obtaining the documents issued in the country of origin, or of shipment, or of both, which the buyer may require either for purposes of exportation, or of importation at destination.

Buyer must

1. Give seller adequate notice of name, sailing date, loading berth of, and delivery time to, the vessel;

2. Bear the additional costs incurred and all risks of the goods from the time when the seller has placed them at his disposal if the vessel named by him fails to arrive or to load within the designated time;

3. Handle all subsequent movement of the goods to destination: (a) provide and pay for insurance; (b) provide and pay for ocean and other transportation;

4. Pay export taxes, or other fees or charges, if any, levied because of exportation;

5. Be responsible for any loss or damage, or both, after goods have been loaded on board the vessel;

6. Pay all costs and charges incurred in obtaining the documents, other than clean ship's receipt or bill of lading, issued in the country of origin, or of shipment, or of both, which may be required either for purposes of exportation, or of importation at destination.

(II-F) "F.O.B." (named inland point in country of importation)"**

Under this term, the seller quotes a price including the cost of the merchandise and all costs of transportation to the named inland point in the country of importation.

Under this quotation:

Seller must

1. Provide and pay for all transportation to the named inland point in the country of importation;

2. Pay export taxes, or other fees or charges, if any, levied because of exportation;

3. Provide and pay for marine insurance;

4. Provide and pay for war risk insurance, unless otherwise agreed upon between the seller and buyer;

5. Be responsible for any loss or damage, or both, until arrival of goods on conveyance at the named inland point in the country of importation;

6. Pay the costs of certificates of origin, consular invoices, or any other documents issued in the country of origin, or of shipment, or of both, which the buyer may require for the importation of goods into the country of destination and, where necessary, for their passage in transit through another country;

7. Pay all costs of landing, including wharfage, landing charges, and taxes, if any;

**See Note (II-A) and Comments on All F.O.B. Terms.

8. Pay all costs of customs entry in the country of importation;

9. Pay customs duties and all taxes applicable to imports, if any, in the country of importation.

NOTE: *The seller under this quotation must realize that he is accepting important responsibilities, costs, and risks, and should therefore be certain to obtain adequate insurance. On the other hand, the importer or buyer may desire such quotations to relieve him of the risks of the voyage and to insure him of his landed costs at inland ports in country of importation. When competition is keen, or the buyer is accustomed to such quotations from other sellers, seller may quote such terms, being careful to protect himself in an appropriate manner.*

Buyer must

1. Take prompt delivery of goods from conveyance upon arrival at destination;

2. Bear any costs and be responsible for all loss or damage, or both, after arrival at destination.

COMMENTS ON ALL F.O.B. TERMS

In connection with F.O.B. terms, the following points of caution are recommended:

1. The method of inland transportation, such as trucks, railroad cars, lighters, barges, or aircraft should be specified.

2. If any switching charges are involved during the inland transportation, it should be agreed, in advance, whether these charges are for account of the seller or the buyer.

3. The term "F.O.B. (named port)," without designating the exact point at which the liability of the seller terminates and the liability of the buyer begins, should be avoided. The use of this term gives rise to disputes as to the liability of the seller or the buyer in the event of loss or damage arising while the goods are in port, and before delivery to or on board the ocean carrier. Misunderstandings may be avoided by naming the specific point of delivery.

4. If lighterage or trucking is required in the transfer of goods from the inland conveyance to ship's side, and there is a cost therefore, it should be understood, in advance, whether this cost is for account of the seller or the buyer.

5. The seller should be certain to notify the buyer of the minimum quantity required to obtain a carload, a truckload, or a barge-load freight rate.

6. Under F.O.B. terms, excepting "F.O.B. (named inland point in country of importation)," the obligation to obtain ocean freight space, and marine and war risk insurance, rests with the buyer. Despite this obligation on the part of the buyer, in many trades the seller obtains the ocean freight space, and marine and war risk insurance, and provides for shipment on behalf of the buyer. Hence, seller and buyer must have an understanding as to whether the buyer will obtain the ocean freight space, and marine and war risk insurance, as is his obligation, or whether the seller agrees to do this for the buyer.

7. For the seller's protection, he should provide in his contract of sale that marine insurance obtained by the

buyer include standard warehouse to warehouse coverage.

(III) F.A.S. (Free Along Side)

NOTE: *Seller and buyer should consider not only the definitions but also the "Comments" given at the end of this section, in order to understand fully their respective responsibilities and rights under "F.A.S." terms.*

"F.A.S. VESSEL (named port of shipment)"

Under this term, the seller quotes a price including delivery of the goods along side overseas vessel and within reach of its loading tackle.

Under this quotation:

Seller must

1. Place goods along side vessel or on dock designated and provided by, or for, buyer on the date or within the period fixed; pay any heavy lift charges, where necessary, up to this point;
2. Provide clean dock or ship's receipt;
3. Be responsible for any loss or damage, or both, until goods have been delivered along side the vessel or on the dock;
4. Render the buyer, at the buyer's request and expense, assistance in obtaining the documents issued in the country of origin, or of shipment, or of both, which the buyer may require either for purposes of exportation, or of importation at destination.

Buyer must

1. Give seller adequate notice of name, sailing date, loading berth of, and delivery time to, the vessel;

2. Handle all subsequent movement of the goods from along side the vessel: (a) arrange and pay for demurrage or storage charges, or both, in warehouse or on wharf, where necessary; (b) provide and pay for insurance; (c) provide and pay for ocean and other transportation;

3. Pay export taxes, or other fees or charges, if any, levied because of exportation;

4. Be responsible for any loss or damage, or both, while the goods are on a lighter or other conveyance along side vessel within reach of its loading tackle, or on the dock awaiting loading, or until actually loaded on board the vessel, and subsequent thereto;

5. Pay all costs and charges incurred in obtaining the documents, other than clean dock or ship's receipt, issued in the country of origin, or of shipment, or of both, which may be required either for purposes of exportation, or of importation at destination.

F.A.S. COMMENTS

1. Under F.A.S. terms, the obligation to obtain ocean freight space, and marine and war risk insurance, rests with the buyer. Despite this obligation on the part of the buyer, in many trades the seller obtains ocean freight space, and marine and war risk insurance, and provides for shipment on behalf of the buyer. In others, the buyer notifies the seller to make delivery along side a vessel designated by the buyer and the buyer provides his own marine and war risk insurance. Hence, seller and buyer must have an understanding as to whether the buyer will obtain the ocean freight space, and marine and war risk insur-

ance, as is his obligation, or whether the seller agrees to do this for the buyer.

2. For the seller's protection, he should provide in his contract of sale that marine insurance obtained by the buyer include standard warehouse to warehouse coverage.

(IV) C. & F. (Cost and Freight)

NOTE: *Seller and buyer should consider not only the definitions but also the "C. & F. Comments" and the "C. & F. and C.I.F. Comments," in order to understand fully their respective responsibilities and rights under "C. & F." terms.*

"C. & F. (named point of destination)."

Under this term, the seller quotes a price including the cost of transportation to the named point of destination.

Under this quotation:

Seller must

1. Provide and pay for transportation to named point of destination;

2. Pay export taxes, or other fees or charges, if any, levied because of exportation;

3. Obtain and dispatch promptly to buyer, or his agent, clean bill of lading to named point of destination;

4. Where received-for-shipment ocean bill of lading may be tendered, be responsible for any loss or damage, or both, until the goods have been delivered into the custody of the ocean carrier;

5. Where on-board ocean bill of lading is required, be responsible for any loss or damage, or both, until the goods have been delivered on board the vessel;

6. Provide, at the buyer's request and expense, certificates of origin, consular invoices, or any other documents issued in the country of origin, or of shipment, or of both, which the buyer may require for importation of goods into country of destination and, where necessary, for their passage in transit through another country.

Buyer must

1. Accept the documents when presented;

2. Receive goods upon arrival, handle and pay for all subsequent movement of the goods, including taking delivery from vessel in accordance with bill of lading clauses and terms; pay all costs of lading, including any duties, taxes, and other expenses at named point of destination;

3. Provide any pay for insurance;

4. Be responsible for loss of or damage to goods, or both, from time and place at which seller's obligations under (4) or (5) above have ceased;

5. Pay the costs of certificates of origin, consular invoices, or any other documents issued in the country of origin, or of shipment, or of both, which may be required for the importation of goods into the country of destination and, where necessary, for their passage in transit through another country.

C. & F. COMMENTS

1. For the seller's protection, he should provide in his contract of sale that marine insurance obtained by the buyer include standard warehouse to warehouse coverage.

2. The comments listed under the following C.I.F. terms in many cases apply to C. & F. terms as well, and should be read and understood by the C. & F. seller and buyer.

(V) C.I.F. (Cost, Insurance, Freight)

NOTE: *Seller and buyer should consider not only the definitions but also the "Comments" at the end of this section, in order to understand fully their respective responsibilities and rights under "C.I.F." terms.*

"C.I.F. (named point of destination)"

Under this term, the seller quotes a price including the cost of the goods, the marine insurance, and all transportation charges to the named point of destination.

Under this quotation:

Seller must

1. Provide and pay for transportation to named point of destination;

2. Pay export taxes, or other fees or charges, if any, levied because of exportation;

3. Provide and pay for marine insurance;

4. Provide war risk insurance as obtainable in seller's market at time of shipment at buyer's expense, unless seller has agreed that buyer provide for war risk coverage (see Comment 10 (c), page 24).

5. Obtain and dispatch promptly to buyer, or his agent, clean bill of lading to named point of destination, and also insurance policy or negotiable insurance certificate;

6. Where received-for-shipment ocean bill of lading may be tendered, be responsible for any loss or damage, or both, until the goods have been delivered into the custody of the ocean carrier;

7. Where on-board ocean bill of lading is required, be responsible for any loss or damage, or both, until the goods have been delivered on board the vessel;

8. Provide, at the buyer's request and expense, certificates of origin, consular invoices, or any other documents issued in the country of origin, or of shipment, or both, which the buyer may require for importation of goods into country of destination and, where necessary, for their passage in transit through another country.

Buyer must

1. Accept the documents when presented;

2. Receive the goods upon arrival, handle, and pay for all subsequent movement of the goods, including taking delivery from vessel in accordance with bill of lading clauses and terms; pay all costs of landing, including any duties, taxes, and other expenses at named point of destination;

3. Pay for war risk insurance provided by seller;

4. Be responsible for loss of or damage to goods, or both, from time and place at which seller's obligations under (6) or (7) above have ceased;

5. Pay the cost of certificates of origin, consular invoices, or any other documents issued in the country of origin, or of shipment, or both, which may be required for importation of the goods into the country of destination and, where necessary, for their passage in transit through another country.

C. & F. AND C.I.F. COMMENTS

Under C. & F. and C.I.F. contracts there are the following points on which the seller and the buyer should be in complete agreement at the time that the contract is concluded:

1. It should be agreed upon, in advance, who is to pay for miscellaneous expenses, such as weighing or inspection charges.

2. The quantity to be shipped on any one vessel should be agreed upon, in advance, with a view to the buyer's capacity to take delivery upon arrival and discharge of the vessel; within the free time allowed at the port of importation.

3. Although the terms C. & F. and C.I.F. are generally interpreted to provide that charges for consular invoices and certificates of origin are for the account of the buyer, and are charged separately, in many trades these charges are included by the seller in his price. Hence, seller and buyer should agree, in advance, whether these charges are part of the selling price, or will be invoiced separately.

4. The point of final destination should be definitely known in the event the vessel discharges at a port other than the actual destination of the goods.

5. When ocean freight space is difficult to obtain, or forward freight contracts cannot be made at firm

rates, it is advisable that sales contracts, as an exception to regular C. & F. or C.I.F. terms, should provide that shipment within the contract period be subject to ocean freight space being available to the seller, and should also provide that changes in the cost of ocean transportation between the time of sale and the time of shipment be for account of the buyer.

6. Normally, the seller is obligated to prepay the ocean freight. In some instances, shipments are made freight collect and the amount of the freight is deducted from the invoice rendered by the seller. It is necessary to be in agreement on this, in advance, in order to avoid misunderstanding which arises from foreign exchange fluctuations which might affect the actual cost of transportation, and from interest charges which might accrue under letter of credit financing. Hence, the seller should always prepay the ocean freight unless he has a specific agreement with the buyer, in advance, that goods can be shipped freight collect.

7. The buyer should recognize that he does not have the right to insist on inspection of goods prior to accepting the documents. The buyer should not refuse to take delivery of goods on account of delay in the receipt of documents, provided the seller has used due diligence in their dispatch through the regular channels.

8. Sellers and buyers are advised against including in a C.I.F. contract any indefinite clause at variance with the obligations of a C.I.F. contract as specified in these Definitions. There have been numerous court decisions in the United States and other countries

invalidating C.I.F. contracts because of the inclusion of indefinite clauses.

9. Interest charges should be included in cost computations and should not be charged as a separate item in C.I.F. contracts, unless otherwise agreed upon, in advance, between the seller and buyer; in which case, however, the term C.I.F. and I (Cost, Insurance, Freight, and Interest) should be used.

10. In connection with insurance under C.I.F. sales, it is necessary that seller and buyer be definitely in accord upon the following points:

a. The character of the marine insurance should be agreed upon in so far as being W.A. (With Average) or F.P.A. (Free of Particular Average), as well as any other special risks that are covered in specific trades, or against which the buyer may wish individual protection. Among the special risks that should be considered and agreed upon between seller and buyer are theft, pilferage, leakage, breakage, sweat, contact with other cargoes, and others peculiar to any particular trade. It is important that contingent or collect freight and customs duty should be insured to cover Particular Average losses, as well as total loss after arrival and entry but before delivery.

b. The seller is obligated to exercise ordinary care and diligence in selecting an underwriter that is in good financial standing. However, the risk of obtaining settlement of insurance claims rests with the buyer.

c. War risk insurance under this term is to be obtained by the seller at the expense and risk of the buyer. It is important that the seller be in definite accord with the buyer on this point, particularly as to the cost. It is desirable that the goods be insured against both marine and war risk with the same underwriter, so that there can be no difficulty arising from the determination of the cause of the loss.

d. Seller should make certain that in his marine or war risk insurance, there be included the standard protection against strikes, riots and civil commotions.

e. Seller and buyer should be in accord as to the insured valuation, bearing in mind that merchandise contributes in General Average on certain bases of valuation which differ in various trades. It is desirable that a competent insurance broker be consulted, in order that full value be covered and trouble avoided.

(VI) EX DOCK

"EX DOCK (named port of importation)"

NOTE: *Seller and buyer should consider not only the definitions but also the "Ex-Dock Comments" at the end of this section, in order to understand fully their respective responsibilities and rights under "Ex Dock" terms.*

Under this term, seller quotes a price including the cost of the goods and all additional costs necessary to place the goods on the dock at the named port of importation, duty paid, if any.

Under this quotation:

Seller must

1. Provide and pay for transportation to named port of importation;

2. Pay export taxes, or other fees or charges, if any, levied because of exportation;

3. Provide and pay for marine insurance;

4. Provide and pay for war risk insurance, unless otherwise agreed upon between the buyer and seller;

5. Be responsible for any loss or damage, or both, until the expiration of the free time allowed on the dock at the named port of importation;

6. Pay the costs of certificates of origin, consular invoices, legalization of bill of lading, or any other documents issued in the country of origin, or of shipment, or of both, which the buyer may require for the importation of goods into the country of destination and, where necessary, for their passage in transit through another country;

7. Pay all costs of landing, including wharfage, landing charges, and taxes, if any;

8. Pay all costs of customs entry in the country of importation;

9. Pay customs duties and all taxes applicable to importers, if any, in the country of importation, unless otherwise agreed upon.

Buyer must

1. Take delivery of the goods on the dock at the named port of importation within the free time allowed;

2. Bear the cost and risk of the goods if delivery is not taken within the free time allowed.

EX DOCK COMMENTS

This term is used principally in United States import trade. It has various modifications, such as "Ex Quay," "Ex Pier," etc., but it is seldom, if ever, used in American export practice. Its use in quotations for export is not recommended.

CHAPTER 10

The Do's and Don'ts of Export

DO

1. Go into export for the long term and plan and act with this in mind.

2. Investigate and learn all you can about export procedures, practices, markets, customs, potential customers, trade leads, information sources and services.

3. Consult with those who can help you.

4. Plan your export program so that you can profitably carry it out.

5. Design, pack and price your product with the same care you use in the domestic market.

6. Use the best talent you can afford to handle your overseas business.

7. Maintain high standards.

8. Advertise and promote as much as you would at home.

DON'T

1. Expect overseas business to come to you more easily than domestic. Both require the same intensive sales cultivation effort.

2. Make the mistake of thinking export is nothing more than "trading beads with the natives." Many people abroad are highly sophisticated and demand the same intelligent approach to business that you'd give your domestic customers.

3. Overlook the need to adapt your product to local overseas requirements.

4. Fail to pack properly to withstand the hazards of transportation and weather.

5. Try to unload products not saleable at home.

6. Avoid business because you may have to extend credit. Check it out thoroughly and you may find that it's well worth it.

7. Forget that you have to conform to the laws of both the United States and the country abroad.

8. Throw away your domestic know-how. Adapt it to meet overseas conditions.